Adelaide
THE Accountant

Wishing you a lasting legacy of peace and prosperity

♡Roslyn

Written by Roslyn Haynie Banks, EA

Illustrated by Bonnie Lemaire

Adelaide the Accountant. Copyright © 2021 by Adelaide Rose, LLC. First printing 2021.

The text of this book is set in Cochin.

ISBN: 978-1-7361942-0-1 Paperback

ISBN: 978-1-7361942-1-8 Hardcover

Library of Congress Control Number: 2021911921

Written by Roslyn Haynie Banks

Edited by Candice L. Davis

Illustrations and cover by Bonnie Lemaire

Published by Adelaide Rose, LLC in Austin, Texas

Cataloging-in-Publication Data has been applied for and may be obtained from the Library of Congress.

I dedicate this book to children, community helpers, accounting professionals, and taxpayers all over the world. It is never too early to begin tax planning strategies and generational transfers of wealth. Wealth includes assets that are tangible and intangible, such as money, property, family values, work ethics, and a good reputation.

"Taxes are very important. We all need to pay our fair share so that we all can succeed!"

I would like to publicly acknowledge and thank my village of family, friends, church members, sorority sisters, educators, mentors, clients, colleagues, and community helpers who have helped me and my children to become better global citizens.

Thank you for purchasing an authentic copy of this publication to sow seeds of financial literacy and accountability to the next generation of world leaders.
-Roslyn

This book was given to:

_____

From:

_____

Occasion or message:

Today is April 1st and Adelaide is excited
about the federal income tax deadline.
She is a tax accountant.
Her job is to save citizens money and time.

"What are taxes? What do they do?"
Well that's a great question.
Let's follow Adelaide.
She will help to guide you.

Adelaide lives in the rural Northern Neck of Virginia,
a farming, fishing, and forestry town.
She helps taxpayers to keep their assets up
and their liabilities down.

On Monday, Adelaide visits a local wellness clinic at noon.
She helps doctors, patients, and instructors pay income taxes.
Those dollars help send astronauts to the moon.

PAYROLL TAXES INCLUDE

SOCIAL SECURITY TAXES

MEDICARE TAXES

UNEMPLOYMENT TAXES

FEDERAL INCOME TAXES

In the studio, her daughters exercise and twirl in ballet class.
Adelaide and the owner discuss payroll taxes for the staff.

Tax dollars help pay for certain types of
medical insurance payments doctors receive.

Taxes are very important.
We all need to pay our fair share
so that we all can succeed!

On Tuesday, Adelaide meets a local farmer,
who stores surplus crops in the grain tanks.
The ladies discuss commodity prices
and year-end account balances at the banks.

Frances wants to invest in solar panels
for a vacant cleared lot.
Her clean, renewable energy sources
will bring in revenue when it's cold and hot.

April is corn planting season.
Adelaide buys a bag of corn seed for her dad.
It is always his one birthday request
and farming as a family makes his heart glad!

On Wednesday, Adelaide goes to the local courthouse
to meet with an official.
Local taxes fund operations for all three government branches –
legislative, executive, and judicial.

The county Treasurer and Board of Supervisors
manage local tax revenue.
Citizens should pay all of their taxes on time
when bills come due.

"But, Adelaide, where does that money go?
Why do my parents have to pay?"
Great question. Taxes also pay for schools and parks
where you can exercise, learn, and play!

On Thursday, Adelaide goes to an
elementary school for career day.
What a wonderful audience!
She listens carefully to what the children have to say.

She answers questions and gives excellent career path advice.
A strong educational foundation
will prepare them to be a future
United States President or Madame Vice.

Adelaide meets with the art teacher to
purchase a unique student creation.
Art, theater, and drama classes are great opportunities
to expand your imagination.

On Friday, Adelaide teaches investor camp
at the local community center.
A financial advisor serves as Adelaide's
business coach and mentor.

Adelaide's magical abacus helps them visualize
debits and credits in groups of ten.
They also discuss financial markets
and what happens when banks lend.

Camp starts with learning the basics
about their local bank.
The high school students can evaluate net present
values and give projects a rank.

On Saturday, Adelaide goes to Williamsburg,
Virginia, for a "mommy and me" play date.
They picnic in the Sunken Gardens,
play frisbee, and roller skate.

On Sunday, they visit the farmer's market
to get fresh produce and lavender soap.
They love supporting other small business owners.
It gives them great hope.

Hope for a thriving economy
for you and for me.
Hope for building generational wealth
to leave a lasting legacy!

Dear readers,

Thank you for supporting my love and passion for the accounting profession! This book was written in response to a Career Day invitation from my childhood elementary school. I wondered, how can I explain taxes and my personal career path to such a young audience?

I attempted to explain a week in the life of a self-employed tax accountant. I tried to connect students with community helper roles they have already explored. I also tried to connect with examples of how their parents and guardians either paid taxes or earned income from tax revenue.

My hope is that this book sows seeds of financial literacy and a sense of community in each reader! It is designed for readers of all ages to be read over and over again as you grow and become more advanced with money and financial literacy concepts.

This book is ideal for bulk graduation gifts, after-school or summer programs, and back-to-school supply drives. Please contact the author directly for bulk purchase discounts and tax-exempt organization sales.

GLOSSARY

ABACUS – a simple manual tool with sliding counters used for addition, subtraction, multiplication and division.

ACCOUNTANT – a person who maintains and interprets financial records. Accountants can work in public accounting firms, governments, not-for-profit organizations, publicly traded companies, or privately-owned businesses.

ACCOUNTING – a process of systematically recording, managing, and presenting financial accounts and transactions. The rules-based system of accounting allows users to monitor and compare financial data including revenue, expenses, and capital. Accounting is also commonly referred to as "the language of business".

ANGEL INVESTOR – a private investor who provides money for small startups or entrepreneurs.

ASSET – a valuable resource that can generate cash flow, reduce expenses, pay debt, or improve sales.

AUDIT – a procedure to determine if a taxpayer correctly reported tax return information and paid the correct amount of tax.

BALANCE SHEET – a financial statement showing a snapshot of what a company owns (assets), owes (liabilities), and the amount invested by owners (equity), at a specific point in time.

CERTIFIED PUBLIC ACCOUNTANT (CPA) – a person who has met all statutory and licensing requirements in the state where he or she works. The CPA designation helps regulate professional standards in the accounting industry. CPAs can provide auditing, bookkeeping, forensic accounting, and managerial accounting services.

COMMODITY – a product or service that is indistinguishable between competitors. Common examples include raw materials such as corn, wheat, sugar, coffee, copper, natural gas, and building supplies.

DEADLINE – a date or time before which something must be done.

ECONOMY – the resources and wealth of a community, typically measured in terms of production and consumption of goods and services.

ENROLLED AGENT (EA) – a person who has earned the privilege of representing taxpayers before the Internal Revenue Service. Enrolled agent status is the highest credential awarded by the IRS. Enrolled Agents must adhere to ethical standards and complete numerous hours of continuing education courses annually.

ENTREPRENEUR – a person who organizes and operates a business with the goal of making a profit by providing products and services to customers.

FINANCE – the study of money, investments, and other financial instruments with the intent to analyze and interpret accounting information to make business decisions.

FINANCIAL ADVISOR – a person who is licensed to provide customized financial counseling and investment advice to individuals for a fee or commission.

FINANCIAL LITERACY – skills and knowledge necessary to understand how money works. Includes concepts of money management, budgeting, saving, investing, lending, and borrowing. Roslyn's goal is that readers will make age-appropriate informed decisions and foster a sense of personal financial well-being.

FINANCIAL MARKETS – a market for the exchange of capital and credit. Examples include stock markets, bond markets, commodities markets, foreign exchange markets, and cryptocurrency markets.

FINANCIAL STATEMENT – a written record showing the financial information of an individual, business, association or government. A complete set of financial statements typically includes a Balance Sheet, Income Statement, and Statement of Cash Flows.

INTERNAL REVENUE SERVICE (IRS) – the United States government agency responsible for the collection of taxes and the enforcement of tax laws. It was founded in 1862, and operates under the authority of the United States Department of the Treasury.

INVESTOR – a person or organization who puts money at risk with the goal of making a profit.

LIABILITY – an obligation to pay money or provide something of value. A financial claim on the assets of a person or organization.

MONEY – legal tender to exchange goods and services. Money includes negotiable instruments such as currency, coins, and checks.

NET PRESENT VALUE (NPV) – a calculation to determine today's value of an investment's net cash inflows and outflows using a given interest rate or required rate of return. An investment is acceptable if the NPV is positive.

PAYROLL TAXES – taxes assessed on the wages, tips, and salaries of employees. The four major types of payroll taxes are income taxes, unemployment insurance, Social Security taxes and Medicare taxes.

REVENUE – total income or cash receipts produced by a given source.

SURPLUS – an excess of what is needed to satisfy immediate needs or demands.

TAX – a fee levied on individuals, corporations, trusts, or estates to pay for government services. Common examples include public works, roads, infrastructure, military protection, schools, and parks.

TAX CREDIT – a dollar-for-dollar reduction in tax liability that is either refundable or non-refundable. Tax credits incent taxpayers to do things that are beneficial for the economy.

TAX DEDUCTION – an expense that reduces taxable income before tax liability is calculated. Common deductions include charitable contributions, mortgage interest paid, and personal property taxes.

TREASURER – a person who is responsible for the receipt, custody, investment, and disbursement of funds.

WEALTH – the value of all assets (tangible and intangible) possessed by a person, family, organization, or country.

Extend the Lesson Activity

Use this space to think about community helpers who work in the science, technology, engineering, arts, and math (STEAM) fields. In this book, we meet five characters who receive and pay income tax dollars to help their local community. Write your thoughts about each character in the space provided. How do they use math at work? How do they earn money?

Adelaide the Accountant

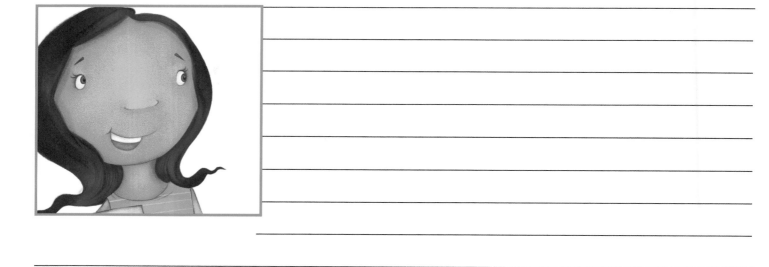

Frances the Farmer

_____
_____
_____
_____
_____
_____
_____
_____
_____

Theresa the Therapist

_____
_____
_____
_____
_____
_____
_____
_____
_____

Elizabeth the Engineer

_____
_____
_____
_____
_____
_____
_____
_____
_____

Alecia the Artist

_____
_____
_____
_____
_____
_____
_____
_____
_____

About the Author:

Roslyn Haynie Banks is an advocate for financial literacy, financial freedom, and fair income tax legislation. She is an accountant, author, and angel investor for kid entrepreneurs. She enjoys teaching children's workshops and coaching taxpayers on strategies to increase their net cash flow. As a federal income tax practitioner, she serves a diverse niche of clients globally, including military service members, veterans, and their families.

Roslyn currently holds an Enrolled Agent (EA) license from the United States Department of the Treasury Internal Revenue Service (IRS). After the annual April 15th tax deadline, she spends countless hours in the summer engaged in continuing education courses on ethics and tax law updates. Becoming an Enrolled Agent or a Certified Public Accountant (CPA) to specialize in income taxation requires a lifelong commitment to learning and serving. She has realized that these unique community helpers truly help to preserve the integrity of worldwide tax systems and the global economy.

While completing her degree in finance from The College of William and Mary, she spent one semester in Adelaide, South Australia, to gain an international vision of the global economy. While obtaining her Masters of Accounting (MAcc) degree, she fell in love with the United States federal income tax system. After her first tax season managing a retail tax office, she passed all three levels of the Enrolled Agent exam on the first try!

Roslyn was born and raised as a fifth-generation farmer on her family farm in the rural Northern Neck of Virginia. She will always have a special appreciation for land ownership – especially since she knows that it is not a depreciable asset! During the global COVID-19 health and economic pandemic, she returned to her hometown to assist with the family farming operations. Roslyn, along with her two daughters were gifted 15 baby chickens from her father in April 2020.

For more information visit www.Hayniebanks.com

About the Illustrator:

Bonnie Lemaire began her career as a freelance illustrator with a promotional post card in 1989. She is a graduate of Ontario College of Art's Communication and Design program, specializing in medical illustration.

Her first position as artist/designer was with Ganz and Brothers Canada, designing figurines and teddy bears! It was a valuable experience, catapulting her into a successful freelance career. She has seen her work utilized in many different projects, including home décor, giftware, stickers, toy design and children's books.

Bonnie's eternal optimism is the foundation of every drawing. Silliness and quirky behavior of those around her are a constant inspiration. Comical and curious characters and creatures come alive and dance on her pages.

Bonnie works in her home studio located in a small Hamlet in Northern Ontario, Canada. Surrounded by her loving family and furry friend Crowquill the studio cat, not to mention 6 quite lively hens cackling away in a converted backyard tree-house chicken coop.

Books she has illustrated have won may awards including; Foreword Clarion 5-Star-Seal, NIEAseal-2014-Winner, and NewPinnacleAward.

Bonnie's eccentric creations within fantastical stories has brought smiles to small faces and delight to her readers all over the world. She continues to enjoy her work, drawing and painting while listening to crime and mystery audio books, Studio Gibli soundtracks and endless reruns of the original Star Trek.

To see more of her work please check out www.bonniella.com